UN/Reconciled

UN/Reconciled

poems of a love gone off

Pasquale Trozzolo

© 2022 Pasquale Trozzolo. All rights reserved.
This material may not be reproduced in any form, published,
reprinted, recorded, performed, broadcast,
rewritten, or redistributed without
the explicit permission of Pasquale Trozzolo.
All such actions are strictly prohibited by law.

Cover design by Shay Culligan
Cover art by William Rose

ISBN: 978-1-63980-212-8

Kelsay Books
502 South 1040 East, A-119
American Fork, Utah 84003
Kelsaybooks.com

> "Tell all the truth
> but tell it slant."
> —Emily Dickinson

Acknowledgments

The author is grateful to the editors of the following journals in which poems of this book previously appeared, sometimes in a slightly different form or with another title:

ASP Bulletin: "How Was Your Day?"
Bluing the Blade: "Old Man and the See"
MONO: "Multitask"
On the Run: "Preface"
Orange Blush Zine: "Crisp"
Red Coyote: "Permission"
Superpresent: "Confess"
Sunspot Literary Journal: "Rumble"
Syncopation Literary Journal: "Loud Music"
Synkroniciti Magazine: "Your Day," "Multitask," "Confess"
Tiny Seed Journal: "Fallen"
Vine Leaves Press: "How Was Your Day?"
Wingless Dreamer: "First Time"

Thank you to my friends and family for indulging my many phases. Special thanks to Becky Blades for making my words better and Marcela Sulak for her thoughtful feedback and encouragement. Thank you to artist William Rose whose art appears on the cover. And thank you to Lisa Phillips and Lindsy Dugan for their assistance. And to my one true love, Joan, there is no poetry without you.

This is a work of fiction. It is not intended to portray any person or combination of persons living or dead—really.

Contents

Preface	11
Forward	12
First Time	13
Change	14
Rumble	15
Unsaved	16
Like Us	17
Multitask	18
How Was Your Day?	19
Accelerating	20
Time	21
Confess	22
Side Effects	23
Over	24
Point of View	25
Therapy	26
Touch	27
UN/Reconciled	28
Whispers	29
Clear	30
Fitting	31
Crisp	32
Mitigate	33
Old Man and the See	34
Happy Hour	35
Loud Music	36
Permission	37
Miss Remembering	38
Fallen	39

Preface

As if something out of a sailor's dream, you walk in, like an actress, superior yet terrified—prey, hunted—eluding. That walk—maybe you were born with it, although likely it's an acquired trait, to complement your red hair and accent. You speak in whispers—another of your movie star tricks, and it works, makes me get close.

Looking like you have something important to say, you charge toward me. Impossible to miss in that mini dress, my eyes follow, like a construction worker. That half-empty bottle of wine you're holding only adds to the allure. Heart pounding, I watch with an accelerating desire, thinking the sort of thoughts that might get me arrested. With no hesitation, you lean in close and whisper, *"Follow me."* Instantly I know I will never forget you.

What started quickly turned into—well, I don't know how to describe it. All I know is that I've been writing poems about you for decades—still, not sure if I'll ever be able to stop or forget. And the truth—I don't want to stop—or forget.

Forward

2:15 a.m.—
why must
even my
dreams be
poems?
Why not
just
dreams?

First Time

In no particular hurry, you clear the clutter of our life: a few dishes, a box of books, our one good painting. You turn to ask a question but stop before you speak. Maybe you're right. All we do is disagree. Not fight. Just disagree. It wasn't always this way.

Doors open. You enter,
capture me like a riptide I can't escape.
Rescue is what I need.

Bronzed was the first
word that came to mind,
though breathless, I could not speak.

The second word
I can't put down for fear of arrest.
Singed, I edge closer.

You're right there—
I can smell you—see you glisten.
As if to invent possibilities

you speak first,
whisper, one word, *"Follow."*
I take your hand

and *follow*. We both
know this is heading for unexplored pleasure.
Days of it. Twenty minutes later

and, already
I know—I'll never
forget you.

Change

At your insistence, we kept things simple, impersonal, focused on fun. Things changed.

I'm just here for fun,
you answer before I even
finish the question. Nonchalantly
you blow smoke softly my way—then kiss
me hard. That was as close to the truth as you got.
You went on to love me, like a gypsy—whenever you
were in town. I waited. Watching you
come and go was almost perfect.
Until you moved in.

Rumble

You always treated our love casually. It seemed easier for you to do things without me. Maybe I was just the object of your play.

You're going off.
Like a ship at sea
you have a melody.
A low rumble
echoing off waves
as if fog were in the air.
You pulse, taking oxygen
as you move. Barely glancing.
Hardly noticing, as if alone.
First I was insulted, but
who am I kidding?
This is meaningless
at its best.

Unsaved

You seemed serious about us for a while, and I was all in. Still, something about you made me feel that I was more in love than you.

Already—it doesn't matter,
I'm in too deep. You are my heroin.
Immediate pleasure followed
by certain pain.
You lure with your sweetness
and kill the future so beautifully.
Yet I chase. Running the fault line
as if nothing will break.

Like Us

Time moved swiftly. Somehow we were "celebrating" two years together. I planned a picnic at the beach. Once we arrived, we found a very private spot and, for about an hour, we enjoyed each other's company. After, we even held hands. Then, in the distance, we heard a single-engine airplane. Just like us, it seemed to struggle.

Impending—
Up and then off
we echo and stall.
It feels like we're about to
come to an abrupt end.
These stunts of ours
scrape the sky with
terror and hope
vibrating through our
own shadows.
A distant but familiar
pulse beckons.
Will we throttle up or
is this the end?

Multitask

We stayed together—almost committed. I was never your priority.

Sounds like you're giving
dictation as we make love
while you talk paint colors and
landscaping. At least you're naked
though covered in your to-do list
and bra. My lover is somewhere
buried in important things too hard to forget
even for the next 12 minutes? You're in a
hurry now, for all the wrong reasons. I want to
complain, but I love you.

How Was Your Day?

Our third anniversary—you greeted me at the door.

All I hear are low notes and misery.
Tell me instead of boats and clouds,
of speed and sex and dreams and bad ideas.
Tell me without the clutter. Be impersonal.
Shocking. Off-kilter. Abduct me with a dangerous tale.
Tell me you like the way I hold my drink.
Touch my hand. Whisper something stirring.
Make me nervous. Be my stranger.
Just for tonight.

Accelerating

Our distance was accelerating with each passing week. Even the few minutes pretending to love each other picked up speed.

Quickly silent.
Minutes ago, you were in full roar,
unafraid of your velocity, accelerating—
in a delicious conversation, with stripped-down words—
faster your favorite, always answered with a well-practiced
rhythm, modulating through an erotic storm of light rain snapping
to dangerous winds. *There,* you say, narrating the journey, as
if guiding lost souls home—*right there.* Dampness cools.
Insatiable turns sleepy. Voluptuous air now
gone, you turn to kiss me—distant again.

Time

As if right on cue, you found a lover, a real gentleman from a few blocks away.

Nothing's wrong,
you said again,
as if this time I
would believe you.
You even added a smile,
a trick that stopped working
about a month ago
when I first saw the texts.
You're good, so is he, apparently.
I guess it's time
to confess. Somehow
I'll be to blame.

Confess

I thought it was my fault. You forgave me.

Your voice scrapes the morning
sunshine into shards of anxiety.
Will you confess again? Make me
hear it all over again? Others
are fooled by your wit and smile
but I know you are dangerous. Your
words soak me in cold—make me damp with
fear—will this be the day? Then you smile.
I'm safe until tomorrow.

Side Effects

After your affair, I came to believe that we would stay together. Be happy together.

Relieved—I believe you.
Why would you lie? Not now, after
all this time together.
Not now—we're vaccinated.
Happy. We made it. No reason
not to believe you.
Yet, I keep searching,
looking for an injury,
almost hoping to find regret.
I smell your hair. Touch it.
It's real. You're *with* me.
You love me.
And even after so much
time together, we're still . . .
Cordial?

Over

Even now, your words hit me like jabs from a prizefighter.

As if I didn't already know
you told me.
I'm not sure why but
it was still a surprise.
The signs were showing
for weeks, maybe longer.
I hoped for less pain
but this trouble moves slowly.
My air is lousy with
your lingering germs.
Months pass, yet my tangled thoughts
raise high on poor attempts to forget.
Painfully similar to yesterday,
I smell you for hours.
Even on this new day
all I see is the morning moon.
Stubborn it hangs
still in the air, barely visible.
Now, just a scarce glow it falls
like me—only seen in the dark.

Point of View

You actually said it—friends. Let's be friends.

There has never been
anything platonic about us.
Come on, you may not be
in love, but platonic?

There is a line, you know.

Just because we never actually
spoke about it does not
mean we did not
cross it.

Therapy

In therapy, we learned lust was our strongest bond.

Here we sit six feet apart,
separated by heat and memories.
Eyes meet—lingering, longing, craving.
It would be nice to meet without the therapy,
with the heat, without the six feet.
Only the indulgence of
accumulated desires.

Touch

The electricity was still there, and I began to hope.

Did we just touch, was that your skin,
did you feel me too?

What should we make of our light touch,
was our brush a sign?

Is this just me still dreaming,
or is there half a chance?

Shall we stand close and risk another or
just walk away?

UN/Reconciled

After the touch, I wanted more, and it felt like you did too.

Exactly. That's what I thought.
We should leave it unexplored. If we
follow this desire all the way, we may find
it's consensual. Unbridled, it could mean trouble.
Perhaps after, we would feel shaken. Even sorrow. It might
not matter, but I'm scared—that you want to say yes, too.
I wonder if these exotic questions are all just
fragments of my dream to touch you in
precisely the right way.

Whispers

After a few texts, I'm hopeful. Maybe you're over him.

Weeks later, we meet for a drink—
I want gin. You want less guilt. You walk
in looking superior yet terrified—like prey, hunted
but eluding—dressed in black. You speak fast and low—
in whispers. Your eyes water—mournful. Like
someone close died. It was then that I noticed—
you're still checking your phone.

Clear

I will always love you, but it was time to go.

Ambiguous—like it's an insult, you accuse me?
Of what—reason, uncertainty?
I don't doubt my guilt, but
who are you to offer interpretation on something
so vague? I find you paradoxical in the extreme,
although mostly just ambivalent about logic. *This*
brings you clarity? That's dubious—
without the high.

Fitting

You continued to call. I continued to resist.

Ironic, your favorite word to misuse
finally fits—a perfect description of
how you loved me but didn't. I tried to
correct you, but you stayed true to your loving
mistake—It is you who suffers now.
I warned you. And yes, you got it right.

Crisp

Finally I realized it was really over. Done. For good.

This time it feels like real winter.
I don't know what happened to the sun.
Just yesterday, it was all daisies.
What changed you?
This storm is at full crisp.
It will not pass easily.
The pain of this cold foretells
my love is gone—for good.

Mitigate

For a long while, all I did was feel sorry for myself. It took a long time to get over you, and I never really got all the way over.

Smooth—a second bottle seems to open itself.
Out pours aloneness, guilt, and an atmosphere
unventilated since you left. I'm drunk
on mysteries of what escaped, staggering in
muck, wondering what turned you,
what doubt swam up—what surfaced to scare you so?
I should have sensed your terror—mitigated.

Old Man and the See

Across a crowded room . . . at an airport . . . in a park . . . without discretion, my imaginary you shows up. My first thought is always "not again," but then happy thoughts take over, and I'm lost.

Like something out of a sailor's dream
she rushes by without so much as a glance.
Despite herculean efforts, she's too much.
My eyes follow, like a construction worker.
As she walks, my heart beats in rhythm to her feet.
Her summer-colored hair waves in sync with
her hands—silk hands.
My thoughts perch on her like the red on her lips.
I swear she is you.
How can it be—so many years past.
Yet still I see you everywhere.
Every bar. Every blonde.
Without warning, she turns, then speaks,
"Can I get you another drink?"
Speechless, I nod a weak yes.

Happy Hour

Yes, I know I should count my blessings. Things turned out pretty well and much better than I deserve. I now seem only to remember you when I'm in the rocks.

Slippery thoughts of you invade my happy hour.
A few cheap gins and I think of you and wonder
do you think back? On nights like this I remember
our first night—and the times before the storm.
As the rounds flow I feel embraced by forgotten vines
squeezing thoughts of you still holding me and I question
Would you feel different? Would there be less pain?
Would our ritual be the same? Would I still be afraid?
Would you still run? Scarcely but still,
I think of you at happy hour.
Do you think back?

Loud Music

It's been decades, yet I can still smell the lemons in your shampoo. Today I heard a distant song, and the notes carried me back to you.

Listening—I hear loud music playing softly
with distant whispers, repeating lyrics—
murmurs of long-exhausted love still beating.
Like a shaken tambourine the rattle
is slightly off-key, background for someone else's song.
Notes play lonely sounds as words escape in
misty layers of dust stirring long-dormant desires.
Barely audible they harmonized—perfect memories
reminding me of lyrics we once sang. Sounds float
lifting my spirits out of range, remembering our love and
songs long over, hoping you sometimes hear
loud music playing softly.

Permission

Sometimes my thoughts of you get so vivid that it feels like I should ask for permission—
I wonder . . . is there anything consensual about these thoughts?

What happens when I
remember you this way?
Can you feel it? Am I bad for it?
This is not an obsession.
You are not on my mind all the time.
I'm not trying to coax you.
I don't want you back.
I really don't want anything more.
Just when I'm alone with my thoughts—
Can I have you?

Miss Remembering

How much is never known?

Sometimes I miss what never was—
Almost remembering what did not
Happen.

Fallen

Sitting under a tree, enveloped by falling leaves, I cried.

You know the sound—
That light scrape of leaf
Once fallen.
Like an old transistor
Radio switched on
It crackles
Passing along the street
With grace and a
Gentle disturbance.
Traveling lightly it
Changes direction
So easily.
Does it know its destination?
Does it know it's
Already dead?
Yet still it travels
And crackles and
Finds me.
I want to follow
But can't keep up, catching
Only fragments.
Does this fallen leaf
Now out of sight know I
Miss her?
I remember how it moved
Sharp, crisp.
And stirring.
And that crackle—
To hear it again
I cry.

About the Author

Pasquale Trozzolo is a retired madman from Kansas. He also spent time as a racecar driver and grad school professor. His poems have appeared in numerous journals and anthologies. The Poetry Box published his debut chapbook, *Before the Distance,* in December 2020. Still no tattoos or MFA, he continues to complicate his life by living out as many retirement clichés as possible.

pasqualetrozzolo.com

www.ingramcontent.com/pod-product-compliance
Lightning Source LLC
Chambersburg PA
CBHW021254200426
R18167700001B/R181677PG43193CBX00001B/1